On Amazon
search:
DiMauro

ISBN 978-0-578-87377-0

DEDICATED

TO MY WIFE

WHOM I LOVE

WHERE DOES YOUR ENERGY ORIGINATE FROM?

WHAT DO
YOU
END UP WITH
IF EVERYTHING
IS GIVEN
TO
YOU?

DOES THE
HEAT AND LIGHT
FROM THE
SUN
GIVE YOU
LIFE?

ARE THE BASIC
NECESSITIES
OF YOUR
LIFE
DERIVED
FROM
NATURE?

WOULD
YOU
BE ALIVE
WITHOUT
IT?

DO YOU FEEL THAT
YOU
HAVE POWER?

DOES THAT POWER
AFFECT
OTHERS?

WHAT DOES IT MEAN
THAT
EVERY ACTION
HAS AN
EQUAL
AND
OPPOSITE
REACTION?

WHAT DOES IT MEAN THAT
ENERGY
IS NEITHER
CREATED
NOR
DESTROYED
ONLY TRANSFORMED?

DO YOU FEEL
NOTHING
BAD
SHOULD EVER
HAPPEN?

TO YOU?

DO YOU BELIEVE IN SLAVERY?

DO YOU BELIEVE IN FREE WILL?

CAN A MIND
BE ENSLAVED
BY
A
CONCEPT
HELD BY
MANY?

ARE YOU JUST A PHYSICAL BODY?

IS SELF-CONTROL SELF-GOVERNANCE?

14

WHAT CAN YOU HOPE FOR FROM A BOOK?

DOES THE VIOLENCE
WITHIN
THE MASSES
DICTATE
WHETHER OR NOT
THERE IS
WAR?

IF PEOPLE
INDIVIDUALLY
CHOOSE
NOT TO
FIGHT
WOULD THERE
BE
WAR?

ARE YOU
AFRAID
TO
LISTEN
TO OTHER
PEOPLES
POINTS
OF VIEW?

DO YOU
FEEL
YOU HAVE
THE RIGHT
TO MAKE
YOUR
OWN
CHOICES?

SHOULD
SOMEONE ELSE
MAKE
THE IMPORTANT
DECISIONS
OF YOUR
LIFE
FOR
YOU?

SHOULD YOU
OR
SOMEONE ELSE
BE
RESPONSIBLE
FOR THE
EFFECTS
OF THE ACTIONS
YOU TAKE?

WHAT IN
LIFE
IMPACTS
YOU THE MOST
WORDS
ACTIONS
OR SOMETHING
ELSE?

HOW DO
YOU
CHANGE
IF AT ALL?

DO YOU WANT TO?

IF YOU DO NOT
FACE
THE
EFFECTS OF YOUR
ACTIONS
OR LACK THERE OF
THEN WHO?

WOULD YOU
LEARN
ANYTHING?

COULD WE
KNOW
LIGHT
WITHOUT
ITS
OPPOSITE?

WITH ONLY
ONE
TYPE OF
EXPERIENCE
IN YOUR
LIFE
COULD YOU
FEEL
ANYTHING?

COULD
YOU
KNOW
YOURSELF
WITHOUT A
REFLECTION?

WHO
OR WHAT
SHOWS
YOU
WHO
YOU ARE?

DID YOU KNOW
THERE IS
A
GRAND PYRAMID
IN THE
STATE
OF
ILLINOIS?

DID YOU KNOW
THAT THE
WALLS
OF A
LOG CABIN
ARE
ALL AT ONCE
INTERIOR SIDING
EXTERIOR SIDING
INSULATION
AND
STRUCTURE?

ARE YOU
AFRAID
OF
BEING
ALONE?

DO YOU FEEL
A
MACHINE
COULD KNOW
YOU
BETTER THAN
YOU
COULD?

DO YOU FEEL
YOU
COULD KNOW
YOURSELF
BETTER
THAN ANYONE
OR
ANYTHING?

CAN YOU
UNDERSTAND
THE
WORD
ARTIFICIAL
AS MEANING
A
FILTER?

HAVE YOU HEARD
THE
SAMURAI
SAY
WHY INSULT
AN
EMPTY
STOMACH
WITH THOUGHTS
OF FOOD?

IF
YOU
WERE NEVER
ALONE
WITH
YOURSELF
COULD YOU
KNOW
YOURSELF?

IF
YOU
ARE ALWAYS
BUSY
COULD YOU
KNOW
YOURSELF?

ARE
YOU
AFRAID
OF
YOURSELF?

HAVE YOU
EVER
STARED
SILENTLY
IN THE
MIRROR
FOR
TEN
MINUTES?

WHY NOT?

DO YOU KNOW
THAT
LISTEN
AND
SILENT
ARE THE
SAME
JUST
REARRANGED?

IS
THAT
ARBITRARY?

IF YOU HAVE
ENERGY
AND YOU
DO NOT CHOOSE
WHERE IT
GOES
WHAT
HAPPENS
TO IT?

CAN
YOU
DETERMINE
WHERE
YOUR ENERGY
GOES?

WHAT IS
VAGUE
IN
YOUR
LIFE?

CAN
YOU
IMAGINE
IT
BEING
ANOTHER WAY?

IF NOT
WHY?

WHERE
DOES
CHANGE
COME FROM?

WHAT HAS
MORE
POWER
THOUGHTS
OR
FEELINGS?

IF
WE CONTROL
SOMETHING
CAN WE
STILL
LOVE
IT
CONSIDERING
IT IS
NO
LONGER
FREE?

IF YOU
ARE
SPOON
FED
ANSWERS
WILL THEY
PRODUCE
LASTING
CHANGE?

HOW CAN
SOMETHING
BE MEANINGFUL
IF YOU
HAVE NOT
SACRIFICED
ANYTHING
FOR IT?

DO YOU
KNOW
THAT
THE
WATER
ON OUR
PLANET
IS IN A
CLOSED
LOOP
SYSTEM?

DO YOU
KNOW
THAT
WATER
HAS
MEMORY?

DO YOU BLAME
OTHERS
FOR THE
STATE
OF THIS
PLANET
ITS
CONDITION?

HAVE YOU CONSIDERED
THE THINGS
YOU
PURCHASE
AFFECT
EVERYTHING
FROM THE
ENVIRONMENT
TO SYSTEMS
OF
GOVERNMENT?

WHAT MUST BE
TAKEN
FOR
AN INDIVIDUAL
IN A
SOCIETY
NOT TO HAVE
POWER
TO CHANGE
THEIR
LIVING
CONDITIONS?

IF
YOU
DO NOT
ACCURATELY
EXPRESS
YOURSELF
HOW CAN YOU
EXPECT
LIFE
TO ORIENT
AROUND YOU
THE WAY YOU
WOULD
LIKE?

IF
IMAGINATION IS POWERFUL
AND
EMOTION IS POWERFUL
WHAT
COULD
NOT BE
CREATED
WHEN AN INDIVIDUAL
COMBINES AND
DIRECTS
THEM?

FOR
PROSPERITY
MUST
ONE
THINK
OF
EVERYTHING?

WHAT ABOUT
WHAT
YOUR
HEART
SAYS?

HAVE YOU
PUT
YOUR
ATTENTION
THERE?

IS NOT
A
QUESTION
A DOORWAY
WALKED THROUGH
WHEN YOUR
INTEREST
IS
SINCERE?

IF SOMETHING
IS GIVEN
AND
YOU
DO NOT
TAKE IT
IS IT
YOURS?

DOES
EVERYONE
FEEL
ABOUT
LIFE
LIKE YOU?

WHY HATE
THE
PROPHETS
WHEN IT IS
THE
PEOPLE
THAT
MISINTERPRET
THEIR
WORDS?

OF ALL
THE HEAVENLY
BODIES
MOVING
THROUGH SPACE
HOW COULD
ONE THINK
OURS
IS THE ONLY ONE
WITH
INTELLIGENT
LIFE?

DOES
THAT NOT
SEEM
A TYPE
OF
NARCISSISM?

WOULD YOU
WITH YOUR SPACE SHIP
WANT TO
VISIT
PLANET EARTH
GIVEN THE
CONDITION
OF THE
PSYCHOLOGY
OF ITS
INHABITANTS?

CAN
EXTERIOR CHANGE
BE
PRODUCED
IF
WITHIN
THERE IS
CONFLICT
PULLING
IN
OPPOSITE
DIRECTIONS?

SHOULD
ONE PERSON
HAVE
THE ENTIRE RESPONSIBILITY
OF
SHARED
LIVING
QUARTERS?

IF YOU
ARE NOT
YOUR THOUGHTS
THEN
COULD THINKING
LEAD YOU
TO
WHAT
YOU
WANT?

CAN A HUMAN
SEAKING
TO
DOMINATE
NATURE
TRULY ADMINISTER
TO A SYSTEM
THAT IS
OF
NATURE?

CAN
NATURE
INCESSANTLY DOMINATED
SUSTAINABLY
PROVIDE?

AT ITS CORE
IS THE
CHILD
A MIRROR
OF THE
PARENT
OR
OF ITS OWN
BEING?

ARE OFFSPRING BOUND TO PARENTS?

IS
LOVE
BINDING?

IS
THERE
FREEDOM
WITHOUT
SOLID
FOUNDATION?

CAN WE
RAISE UP
OFF THE FLOOR
IF WE
DO NOT
PUSH
OR
IF THERE WERE
NO
FLOOR?

DO YOU KNOW OF NUNCHI?

CAN YOU
IMAGINE
THE
RAMIFICATIONS
IF
EVERYONE
CLEANED UP
THEIR
OWN
MESS?

WHAT OF
YOURS
DO
YOU
LEAVE
FOR OTHERS
TO CLEAN UP
WITHOUT
COMPENSATING?

IF
SOME THING
IS NOT
VALIDATED
BY
SCIENTIFIC PROOF
OR
UNIVERSITY STUDIES
DOES THAT MEAN
IT
IS YET
TO BE
TRUE?

IS THERE
REAL
HAPPINESS
WITHOUT
WORK
OR
EFFORT?

IS THERE
UNITY
IN
LIFE
OR
RANDOM
ISOLATED
EVENTS?

DO
PEOPLE
ALL
FUNDAMENTALLY
WANT
THE
SAME
THINGS?

HOW
DO YOU
WANT
TO BE
WHEN
YOU
DIE?

DO
YOU
WANT TO BE
THAT
WAY
NOW?

WHY
WEAR PLASTIC
WHEN
YOU CAN WEAR
WOOL?

IF WE
DO
NOT
TAKE CARE OF
OUR OWN
NEEDS
ARE WE
CREATING
A MESS
FOR SOMEONE ELSE
TO
CLEAN UP?

SHOULD WE
MAKE
WAR
IN THE NAME
OF
PEACE?

CAN YOU MAKE
ICE
WITH A
MATCH?

DO WE HAVE THE RIGHT TO DEFEND OURSELVES?

ARE RELIGIOUS TEACHINGS
THEMSELVES
WRONG
CONSIDERING
IT IS
PEOPLE
THAT
CHOOSE TO
MISUSE
THEM FOR
SELFISH
PURPOSES?

CAN YOU
TRULY
BE AN
ADVOCATE OF PEACE
WITHOUT THE
CAPACITY
TO
LISTEN TO
AND UNDERSTAND
OPPOSING POINTS
OF
VIEW?

CAN
YOU UNDERSTAND
SOMETHING
YOU
DO NOT
AGREE
WITH
OR
THAT
MAKES YOU
UNCOMFORTABLE?

IS IT HEALTHY
TO
POOP
LESS THAN
ONCE
A DAY?

WHAT DO
PEOPLE
WITH
POLARIZED CONCEPTS
OF
SCIENCE
RELIGION
POLITICS
ETCETERA
ACCOMPLISH?

DO YOU
KNOW
ANYTHING
OF THE
LAST TWO THOUSAND
YEARS
OF
HUMAN
HISTORY?

DO
YOU
APPRECIATE
WHEN YOU
ARE
TOLD
THE
TRUTH?

DO PEOPLE
HAVE
A TENDENCY
TO REPEAT
THEMSELVES
WHEN THEY DO NOT
REMEMBER
WHAT
THEY HAVE
SAID
OR
DONE?

WHO
BENEFITS
FROM
DESTROYING
REMIDERS
OF
PAST
MISTAKES?

DO YOU FEEL
THE
PREVALENCE
OF ART
FULL OF
VIOLENCE
DISCORDANCE
ETCETERA
CONDUCIVE TO
THE
UPLIFTING
OF A
CULTURE?

HOW DO YOU
DO
OTHER THAN
THAT
WHICH IS
RIGHT
IN FRONT
OF YOU?

IS IT DONE WELL?

DO YOU
EVER
LOOK
TO WHERE
THE
DIRECTION
OF THE
TRAIL
YOU ARE LEAVING
IS
HEADED?

AT NIGHT
WHY DOES THE LIGHT
FROM STARS
TWINKLE
WHEREAS
THE LIGHT
FROM PLANETS
IS
FIXED?

WHY DOES DEATH SCARE PEOPLE?

DOES
THINKING
WE
KNOW
SOMETHING
HAVE ANYTHING
TO DO WITH
THAT
WHICH IS
TRUTH?

DOES
EVOLUTION
MEAN
WE BECOME
MORE AND MORE
DEPENDENT
ON
SOMETHING
OUTSIDE
OURSELVES?

HOW CLOSE
IS THE
RELINQUISHING
OF FREEDOM
TO
BEING
AN ACCOMPLICE
TO SLAVERY?

DOES
A LACK
OF CARING
ARISE
FROM
OVERSTIMULATION?

DO YOU
FIND
THE CURRENT
STATE OF YOUR WORLD
APPEALING?

WHEN WAS THE
LAST TIME
YOU
MADE A DECISION
THAT WAS
NOT
IN ITS DEPTH
BASED
IN FEAR?

DO NOT THE ADHERENTS
OF BOTH
ATHEISM AND RELIGION
SEEK SOLACE
FROM THE UNKNOWN
BY WAY OF
SCIENCE
OR
DOGMA?

IF THERE ARE
NO PEOPLE
IS THERE
LIFE
OR
TRUTH?

IS THERE
ANY HOPE
FOR A PERSON
WHO CHOOSES
TO REMAIN IGNORANT
OTHER
THAN TO END UP
A
SLAVE?

WHAT IS
THE
MORE EFFECTIVE
FORM OF
SLAVERY
PHYSICAL
OR
MENTAL-EMOTIONAL?

DO YOU
HAVE
IGNORANCE
THAT OTHERS
ARE
CAPITALIZING
UPON?

WITHOUT PURPOSE
ARE WE NOT
EASILY
SWAYED?

WHAT HAS PREVENTED
YOU FROM
ASKING
THESE QUESTIONS
OF YOURSELF
YOURSELF?

DO YOU
EVER
STOP?

DO YOU
DESIRE
OTHER THAN
PEACE AND HAPPINESS?

DO OTHERS?

WHAT REASON IS THERE
TO SACRIFICE
FOR THE
PERPETUATION
OF THAT WHICH IS
DEVOID
OF
VIRTUE?

WERE THE
MANY
ASKED
IF THEY WANTED
A FEW
SACRIFICED
FOR
THEM?

DO YOU HAVE
ANY
MEANS OF
PERCEPTION
OTHER THAN
YOUR FIVE SENSES?

WITH
WHAT DO YOU
SEE
YOU
DREAMS?

ARE DISCOVERY AND
COMPREHENSION
THE SAME?

DOES THE FORMER
AUTOMATICALLY
CONFER
THE
LATER?

SINCE
QUANTUM PHYSICS
FINDS
ALL
POSSIBLE
SIMULTANEOUSLY
HOW IS IT
THAT
GOD
DOES NOT
EXIST?

WHAT
IS THE REASON
FOR
ARGUING
ABOUT IT?

AS THE
SUN STREAMS
THROUGH
MY
WINDOW
WHO
COULD DENY
IT
A HOME?

WHAT SHALL
WE DO
WITH
YOUR LEAST
FAVORITE COLORS?

AND YOUR
FAVORITES?

IF
WE ARE SO MUCH
MORE
EVOLVED
THAN THEY WERE
HOW IS THERE
MACHU PICCHU
TEOTIHUACAN
THE GIZA COMPLEX
ALL STILL
STANDING?

WHY SUCH
FOCUS
ON THE
PEAK OF THE MOUNTAIN
WHILST THERE IS
LITTLE
JOY
DERIVED FROM
KEEPING
OUR BOWLING BALL
OUT
OF THE GUTTER?

IS NOT
THE UNKNOWN
FROM
WHERE
FREEDOM
COMES TO
US?

Made in the USA
Monee, IL
01 April 2021